Mountain Birds of the West

Genevieve Einstein
& Einstein Sisters

KidsWorld

Quick Guide

These are some of the birds that you are most likely to see in the mountains of Western North America. We've included their measurements in case you want to have fun with rulers!

Harlequin Duck p. 8
Length: 15 in (39 cm)

Common Merganser p. 10
Length: 25 in (63 cm)

White-tailed Ptarmigan p. 12
Length: 12 in (30 cm)

Dusky Grouse p. 14
Length: 20 in (51 cm)

Broad-tailed Hummingbird p. 16
Length: 4 in (10 cm)

Spotted Sandpiper p. 18
Length: 7 in (18 cm)

California Gull p. 20
Length: 20 in (51 cm)

Osprey p. 22
Length: 22 in (56 cm)

Golden Eagle p. 24
Length: 30 in (77 cm)

**Sharp-shinned
Hawk p. 26**
Length: 11 in (28 cm)

**Northern
Goshawk p. 28**
Length: 23 in (59 cm)

**Red-tailed
Hawk p. 30**
Length: 22 in (56 cm)

Great Gray Owl p. 32
Length: 29 in (73 cm)

Boreal Owl p. 34
Length: 10 in (25 cm)

**Belted
Kingfisher p. 36**
Length: 13 in (32 cm)

**Williamson's
Sapsucker p. 38**
Length: 9 in (23 cm)

Northern Flicker p. 40
Length: 12 in (30 cm)

**Peregrine
Falcon p. 42**
Length: 17 in (43 cm)

Red-eyed Vireo p. 44
Length: 5 in (13 cm)

Canada Jay p. 46
Length: 11 in (28 cm)

Steller's Jay p. 48
Length: 13 in (32 cm)

Clark's Nutcracker p. 50
Length: 11 in (28 cm)

Common Raven p. 52
Length: 25 in (63 cm)

Horned Lark p. 54
Length: 7 in (18 cm)

Cliff Swallow p. 56
Length: 5 in (13 cm)

Mountain Chickadee p. 58
Length: 5 in (13 cm)

Bushtit p. 60
Length: 3 in (8 cm)

Red-breasted Nuthatch p. 62
Length: 4 in (10 cm)

Pygmy Nuthatch p. 64
Length: 4 in (10 cm)

Brown Creeper p. 66
Length: 5 in (13 cm)

Rock Wren p. 68
Length: 6 in (15 cm)

American Dipper p. 70
Length: 7 in (18 cm)

Ruby-crowned Kinglet p. 72
Length: 4 in (10 cm)

**Mountain
Bluebird p. 74**

Length: 7 in (18 cm)

**Townsend's
Solitaire p. 76**

Length: 8 in (21 cm)

**Evening
Grosbeak p. 78**

Length: 7 in (18 cm)

Pine Grosbeak p. 80

Length: 9 in (23 cm)

House Finch p. 82

Length: 6 in (15 cm)

Pine Siskin p. 84

Length: 5 in (13 cm)

**Dark-eyed
Junco p. 86**

Length: 6 in (15 cm)

**White-crowned
Sparrow p. 88**

Length: 6 in (15 cm)

Spotted Towhee p. 90

Length: 7 in (18 cm)

**Brewer's
Blackbird p. 92**

Length: 9 in (23 cm)

**Wilson's
Warbler p. 94**

Length: 4 in (10 cm)

How to Use this Book

Each bird in this book has icons in the right-hand corner. These icons quickly tell you the size of the bird, where to look for it, what food it eats and what kind of nest it builds.

Size

Small is for birds that are shorter than the length of a school ruler (1 ft/30 cm).

Medium is for birds that are between one and two school rulers long (1-2 ft/30-60 cm).

Large is for birds that are bigger than two school rulers placed end to end (2 ft/60 cm).

Where to Look

 On or close to the ground

 On or close to the water

 In trees or shrubs

 In the air

Food

 Seeds, flowers or other plant parts

 Fruits or berries

 Insects or other creepy crawlies

 Fish or other water animals

 Land animals (like mice) or birds

Nests

Simple nests are often on the ground. Birds don't put much effort into simple nests.

Cup-shaped nests are usually found in trees. These are often made with grass and twigs.

Some birds like to nest in tree cavities or nest boxes.

Some birds have nests that are unusual. They don't fit into the other categories.

Harlequin Duck

The Harlequin Duck comes to the mountains in the spring to raise its young. In the fall it returns to rocky ocean shores.

Harlequin Ducks talk to each other with mouse-like squeaks. One nickname for this duck is sea mouse. Other nicknames include rock ducks and lords and ladies.

Harlequin Ducks may look fancy, but they are also tough. They are often thrown around in the rough waters of fast-moving rivers. Many birds break a bone at some point in their lives.

The Harlequin Duck can dive into water from the air! It can also go directly into flight from under the water.

Common Merganser

Sawbill is one of the nicknames for the Common Merganser. Its bill has sharp tooth-like ridges. The jagged bill edge helps it catch and hold onto fish.

The Common Merganser's favorite food is fish, especially salmon. It catches fish and water bugs when it dives under the water.

Other birds often try to steal the fish this bird catches! Gulls, Bald Eagles and other mergansers are the most common thieves.

Within two days of leaving the nest, chicks can dive and catch food on their own. They listen for their mother's alarm call to warn them of danger.

11

White-tailed Ptarmigan

The White-tailed Ptarmigan lives above the treeline. It is the only bird in North America that stays high up in the mountains all year long.

During the day, the White-tailed Ptarmigan digs a hole in snow as a resting place. At night, it may sleep under the snow!

In the winter, the layer of feathers on this bird's legs gets thicker. The extra feathers keep the ptarmigan's feet warm and also act like snowshoes.

Hatchlings leave the nest the day they hatch. When their mom finds food, she makes a special sound. The call tells the chicks to look for food where she is pecking at the ground.

13

Dusky Grouse

In the fall, this bird swallows small stones that stay in its stomach for months. The stones grind together to help break down the tough conifer needles it eats during the winter.

Cats aren't the only animals that purr. The female Dusky Grouse makes a purring sound while her eggs are hatching!

In the spring, males fan their tail feathers while displaying their red neck patches. They also make grunting hooting sounds. They do all this to attract females and to claim their territory.

Q: What do you call a funny female grouse?
A: A comidi-hen!

15

Broad-tailed Hummingbird

Broad-tailed Hummingbirds live in mountain meadows and open forests from May to August. They spend the rest of the year in Mexico.

Broad-tailed Hummingbirds are like little mountain fairies. They flit from flower to flower, drinking nectar. Their wings even make a tinkling sound as they fly!

Hummingbirds have short legs and small feet.
This helps keep their body weight light for easier flying.
It also means they can't walk or hop.

Spotted Sandpiper

The Spotted Sandpiper is found on the shores of mountain lakes and rivers. It often makes *weet-weet* calls as it walks or flies.

The Spotted Sandpiper bobs its body up and down when walking or standing. This behavior, called teetering, has earned it many nicknames, like teeter-tail.

The female lays up to five eggs in the nest she builds with the male. She lays one egg per day. Five eggs together weigh as much as she does!

Chicks start teetering as soon as 30 minutes after they hatch! They start catching their own food at only one or two days old.

19

California Gull

This white-headed gull has both a black and a red mark on its yellow bill. It also has a gray back and yellow legs.

In the fall and winter this bird has grayish streaks on its head.

These gulls spend the winter along the Pacific Coast. They come to the mountains in the spring to raise their young. They make their nests on islands in lakes or rivers.

California Gulls are talkative birds.
They live in groups and spend a lot of time talking
to each other with their loud calls!

Q: Why do
seagulls like to live
by the sea?
A: Because if they lived
by the bay they would
be called bay-gulls
(bagels)!

21

Osprey

Fifty years ago, chemicals meant to kill insects were causing Osprey eggs to be weak and nestlings to get sick. These chemicals aren't being used anymore, so Osprey populations are growing in numbers again.

The Osprey is also known as fish hawk. It snatches fish from the water with its strong talons. The soles of its feet have sharp scales to help grip its slippery prey.

When the male catches a fish, he brings it to the nest. He eats the head of the fish and then gives the rest of the fish to the female. She feeds the chicks and herself.

23

Golden Eagle

The Golden Eagle is a fierce hunter. It eats rabbits, squirrels and birds that it kills with its sharp talons. Sometimes it even hunts larger animals, like foxes or deer.

Sometimes the Golden Eagle dives from a great height in the sky. When it dives, it can reach speeds around 200 mph (320 km/h), which is almost as fast as a Formula One race car!

The Golden Eagle finds its prey with its keen eyesight. It has better vision than people do and can see more colors, too. It can see pee trails that other animals leave behind, which can help the bird find them.

For the first month, nestlings spend a lot of time sleeping. They sleep on their belly. When they are older, nestlings back up to the edge of the nest to poop.

Sharp-shinned Hawk

The Sharp-shinned Hawk is one of the smallest hawks in North America. This hawk gets its name from its long, slender yellow legs.

This hawk hunts mostly birds. Unlike some birds of prey, it plucks the feathers off its meal before eating it.

The female is larger than the male and hunts larger birds. This size difference is obvious even in Sharp-shinned Hawk chicks that are only a week old.

Chicks start to leave the nest when they are 4 weeks old. For the first month after chicks leave the nest, parents pass food to them in mid-air!

Northern Goshawk

Originally, the Northern Goshawk was called goose hawk. Over time the name changed into goshawk. This large hawk eats bigger birds, like geese and ducks. It also eats squirrels and rabbits.

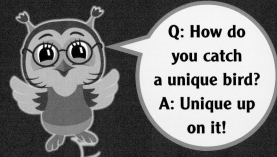

Q: How do you catch a unique bird? A: Unique up on it!

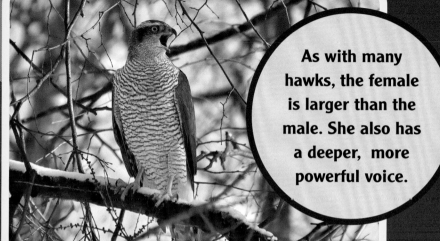

As with many hawks, the female is larger than the male. She also has a deeper, more powerful voice.

The Northern Goshawk typically nests in the tallest tree in its territory. It attacks animals, including people, that get too close to its nest.

29

Red-tailed Hawk

This hawk gets its reddish tail in its second year of life. Other than the tail, the overall look of the bird varies a lot, with light morph and dark morph birds.

The screeching call of the Red-tailed Hawk is often used in movies. It is usually the sound used for any hawk or eagle in Hollywood films.

The Red-tailed Hawk is a sit-and-wait predator. It spends a lot of time on a high perch, looking for its next meal.

At 3 weeks old, chicks can defend themselves against nest intruders. They leave the nest for the first time when they are around 6 weeks old.

31

Great Gray Owl

Also called the Bearded Owl, the Great Gray Owl looks like it has a white mustache and a black bow tie. It is the largest owl in North America.

This owl has super hearing! The large facial discs around its eyes help send sound waves to its ears. It can hear movements of animals the length of a soccer field away.

The Great Gray Owl flies silently on its broad wings with slow wing beats. Its strong talons can snatch mice from under the snow or even gophers from their burrows!

As with many owls, this bird's left ear and right ear are at different heights on its head. This helps it find animals using sound alone.

Boreal Owl

The Boreal Owl hunts small animals at night. Females are larger than males and can weigh twice as much!

The male finds tree cavities and sings inside them to attract the female. The female decides which cavity she will use for nesting.

The Boreal Owl sleeps in the daytime.
It sleeps close to the trunk of a tree, and it chooses a new sleeping spot every day.

At about one month old, chicks leave the nest. They then stay together in a loose group for a week or more.

Belted Kingfisher

The Belted Kingfisher hunts for fish near mountain rivers and lakes. It swallows the fish whole, head first. Then later it spits out the bones and scales as a pellet.

This kingfisher watches the water from a perch or hovers over the water. When it sees a fish swimming near the surface, it swoops down and catches the fish in its bill.

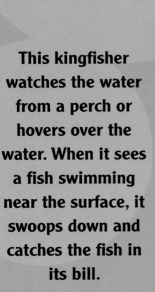

The kingfisher has webbing between some of its toes. The webbing helps its feet work like shovels when it digs its nest tunnel into a riverbank.

Here is an example of what is believed to be a Kingfisher's nest.

37

Williamson's Sapsucker

The Williamson's Sapsucker makes shallow holes in trees with its bill. Then it licks the tree sap that flows out, as well as the insects stuck in the sap. A group of sapsuckers is called a slurp of sapsuckers!

The female and male look so different that for a long time they were thought to be different species. Even as nestlings, males and females look different.

Young males lack the red chin and yellow belly of adult males. They quickly learn how to find food and love to eat ants!

39

Northern Flicker

The Northern Flicker uses its strong bill to hammer into soil, instead of trees. Its favorite food is ants. It can often be found dining at anthills!

Northern Flickers in western North America have red feathers on their wings. Birds in the east have yellow feathers. The Rocky Mountains are home to both red-shafted and yellow-shafted birds.

The female lays eggs on woodchips at the bottom of its cavity nest. The male and female take turns incubating the eggs and feeding the nestlings.

41

Peregrine Falcon

The Peregrine Falcon hunts mostly birds. It has amazing vision and can spot prey more than 30 football fields away (1.8 miles, 3 km).

The Guinness World Record for fastest bird goes to the Peregrine Falcon. It was recorded at 242 mph (389 km/h) while diving in flight. That's faster than most race cars can go!

In the mountains, the Peregrine Falcon usually nests on a cliff. It mates for life and often uses the same nest site many years in a row.

Chicks start to peep inside the egg up to 3 days before they hatch. Parents sometimes help remove egg shells in the later stage of hatching.

Red-eyed Vireo

The Red-eyed
Vireo eats mostly
insects in the summer.
This bird spends the
winter in South America
where it eats
mostly fruit.

This bird's
eyes don't
turn red until it
is about 9 or
10 months old.

This bird's song sounds like it is asking a question and answering it, over and over again. One male was recorded singing over 20,000 songs in one day!

The female builds the nest by herself. She collects sticky spider webs in her bill and uses them to glue the nest materials together.

Canada Jay

The Canada Jay (also known as Camp Robber) is a common campsite thief in the mountains. It will also eat food right out of people's hands or pots! It eats almost anything!

Until 2018, this bird was known as the Gray Jay. It is also known as the Whisky Jack. Like most jays, it is friendly and very clever. A group of jays is called a party of jays.

In the summer and fall, the Canada Jay stores food in trees. It glues food to branches with its sticky saliva. In the winter when food is hard to find, it dines on these ready snacks.

The Canada Jay is one of the few birds that nests in the winter. It incubates eggs when the weather is as cold as -22°F(-30°C)!

47

Steller's Jay

The Steller's Jay is a beautiful bird and also a great mimic. This bird can imitate a wide range of sounds of other animals or devices, including cats, dogs, chickens, other birds and even telephones!

The crest on this bird's head shows how it feels. When the bird is relaxed, the crest is down. When the bird is angry, scared or excited, the crest raises up.

When they are just a few months old, these jays are mostly gray with blue wings and tail. Young birds may stay with their parents until winter.

Clark's Nutcracker

The **Clark's Nutcracker** hangs out in high mountain forests. Sometimes a large flock (flock) of nutcrackers gathers to feed together.

This bird's favorite food is pine cones. It holds the cone with its foot and jabs between the scales with its long bill to get the seeds.

The Clark's Nutcracker hides seeds. It buries them underground or stuffs them in cracks in trees. This bird also has a pouch under its tongue where it can carry 100 seeds or more at a time!

This bird has an amazing memory. It usually remembers where all of its seeds are hidden. If it ever forgets about an underground seed stash, the seeds will grow into new trees!

Common Raven

The **Common Raven** is the largest songbird in the world! It is also super smart, just like crows and parrots.

Q: What is even smarter than a talking bird?
A: A spelling bee!

The Common Raven is an acrobat in flight. It can do stunts like rollovers in the air. One funny bird was seen flying upside down for a long distance!

Common Ravens are able to imitate all kinds of sounds. When raised by humans, they can mimic human speech, like parrots do!

53

Horned Lark

The male Horned Lark has black tufts that look like horns on the top of his head. The female has no tufts and fainter markings.

The Horned Lark lives in open areas with few trees. In the mountains, it nests in alpine meadows.

In the fall and winter, Horned Larks sometimes gather in large flocks. A flock is called a **happiness** of larks.

When a chick poops, the poop is wrapped in a thin skin sac. The parent keeps the nest clean by taking the poop sac in its bill and dropping it on the ground away from the nest.

Cliff Swallow

The Cliff Swallow can be found on the lower parts of mountains. It catches flying insects while it flies over open areas.

The Cliff Swallow uses balls of mud to build its nest. It carries mud in its bill then it adds dry grass to line the nest.

This bird builds its nests in large groups on the sides of cliffs and sometimes on buildings.

Mountain Chickadee

The Mountain Chickadee is one of the most common birds in mountain forests. When you hear its *chick-a-dee-dee* call, you will understand where its name comes from!

This bird gets water from the food it eats. It will drink from a stream or lake when it can. It also likes to take a bath in water, or even in snow!

In the winter, the Mountain Chickadee sometimes sleeps in a tree cavity to keep warm. Usually it sleeps on its own, but sometimes a pair will sleep in the same cavity.

59

Bushtit

The lively **Bushtit** flits through mountain trees looking for insects and spiders. In the summer it lives high up in the mountains. In the winter it moves to lower mountain slopes.

Bushtits often gather in flocks. On cold nights, they huddle together to keep warm.

The Bushtit builds a sock-like hanging nest as long as a school ruler. The nest can take more than a month to build!

Female Bushtits have pale eyes. Males and juveniles have dark eyes.

Red-breasted Nuthatch

The Red-breasted Nuthatch is found in spruce and fir forests. It climbs down tree trunks head first, searching for insects that are its favorite summer food.

The Red-breasted Nuthatch carves its own nest hole. It smears the nest opening with sticky tree resin. It avoids the resin by flying right through the nest hole!

This bird eats mostly conifer seeds in the fall and winter. In the summer, it hides seeds for the colder months. It usually hides these food caches under bark, in tree holes or in the ground.

Pygmy Nuthatch

The **Pygmy Nuthatch** is just as comfortable upside down as it is right side up. Its high-pitched *peep* call is like the sound a rubber ducky makes when it is squeezed.

These avian busybodies are often found in groups. In the winter they sleep together in large groups in tree cavities. One biologist saw more than 100 birds fit into a single tree cavity!

The Pygmy Nuthatch eats a lot of insects. It isn't afraid of spiders or wasps and will eat them for lunch!

Q: Why did the little bird get in trouble at school? A: Because it was caught tweeting on a test!

65

Brown Creeper

The **Brown Creeper** spirals its way up the biggest trees in the forest. Its song sounds like a whistled *trees, beautiful trees!*

The Brown Creeper's favorite food is insects. Trees with deep grooves in the bark usually have the most insects hiding in them. The creeper's long bill helps it reach these hidden bugs.

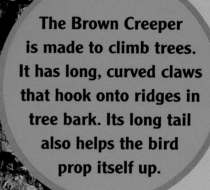

The Brown Creeper is made to climb trees. It has long, curved claws that hook onto ridges in tree bark. Its long tail also helps the bird prop itself up.

The Brown Creeper has an unusual nest. It is built behind a peeling piece of bark.

Rock Wren

Rock Wrens are generally found in dry areas. Their bodies are good at getting all the water they need from their food. When they are offered water in captivity, they have no interest in it.

The male Rock Wren is a talented singer. He may sing up to 20 songs per minute, choosing from over 100 different song types!

The Rock Wren builds its nest in a cavity in or among rocks. The young are fed mostly grasshoppers, crickets and moths.

American Dipper

The American Dipper is found along mountain streams. It eats water bugs and small fish that hang out near rocky stream bottoms.

Q: What bird loves guacamole?
A: The Dipper!

This bird is called a Dipper because it dips its head underwater to catch food. It has clear eyelids that act like goggles. It also has a flap that closes its nostrils when it is underwater.

The American Dipper weaves a ball-like nest from grass and moss. It dips the nesting materials in water before using them to make the nest.

Ruby-crowned Kinglet

Ruby-crowned Kinglets are very small birds, even smaller than chickadees. They flick their wings almost constantly, which is one way to recognize them.

The male's ruby red crown is easy to see when he sings in the spring. Spring is an exciting time because it is when he finds his mate.

The Ruby-crowned Kinglet's nest is well hidden near the tree trunk. The female can lay up to 12 eggs, which is a lot for a bird of her size!

Mountain Bluebird

The Mountain Bluebird is one of the first birds to return to the mountains in the spring. It wants to have first choice of tree cavity nesting sites, which can be in short supply.

The female chooses her mate based on how much she likes the nesting site he picks. As she builds the nest, she sometimes adds feathers to it.

As early as 14 days old, males have more blue in their feathers than females. Young birds are fed mostly beetles and grasshoppers.

75

Townsend's Solitaire

The **Townsend's Solitaire** spends its time around the treeline on mountains in the summer. It makes its nest on the ground and eats insects, especially caterpillars, ants and beetles.

This bird sings to defend its territory. The song is complex, and both males and females sing. In some songbirds only males sing.

In the winter, the Townsend's Solitaire moves to an area rich in juniper berries. It fiercely defends its territory of juniper trees because the berries are its main food for the winter.

Evening Grosbeak

The Evening Grosbeak brings a splash of sunshine to mountain forests year-round. The female is duller than the flashy male but still has yellow on her neck and shoulders.

Evening Grosbeaks gather in big flocks in the winter. They like seeds and cones that they easily crack open with their large bills!

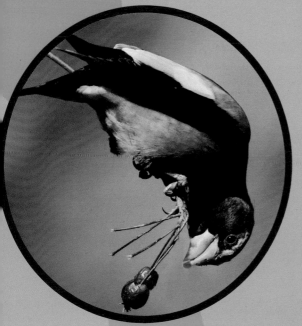

When people eat fruits with pits, they eat the flesh and throw away the pit. The Evening Grosbeak does the opposite! It is most interested in the hard seed inside the fruit.

Pine Grosbeak

The **Pine Grosbeak** is most common in open conifer forests near the treeline. It is the largest of the northern finches. Like other finches it has a big, thick bill.

This bird uses its strong bill to crack open seeds and nip fresh buds off trees. It also likes berries and other fruits.

The Pine Grosbeak has a thick coat of feathers to help keep it warm in the winter. The bright red male is easy to spot in the snow.

81

House Finch

The male House Finch gets his color from chemicals in the foods he eats. The female likes to mate with the reddest male she can find.

The House Finch often returns to the same place every year to raise its young. It starts mating the first spring after it is born and can live up to 11 years in the wild.

Most females lay eggs more than once each year. The male takes care of the chicks from the first nest when they are ready to fly. Then the female lays another set of eggs.

83

Pine Siskin

The **Pine Siskin** is often seen at the tops of trees. One of its favorite foods is seeds. It hangs upside down to get seeds out of conifer cones.

Q: How do birds pay at a restaurant? A: With their bills!

This bird looks really plain until it takes flight. Then you can see the flash of yellow on its wings and tail.

The Pine Siskin can store seeds in its crop, which is a pouch in its throat. It can store enough seeds to survive five hours of freezing temperatures overnight.

85

Dark-eyed Junco

The Dark-eyed Junco is one of the most common birds in North America. It is nicknamed snowbird because it often shows up at birdfeeders in the winter.

This bird comes in many different color patterns. In all forms, it has a dark hood over its head and neck, and white feathers on the outside of its tail.

The Dark-eyed Junco usually makes its nest on the ground. Some juncos make simple nests, while others put a lot of work into them.

White-crowned Sparrow

The White-crowned Sparrow hops on the ground looking for seeds and insects. In the winter it flocks together to form a flutter of sparrows.

Q: Why do birds sing in the morning?
A: Because they don't have to go to school!

The young male learns to sing by the time he is 3 months old. He learns by listening to neighboring males. Songs vary from region to region.

Adults have black and white stripes on their heads. Young birds have brown and gray stripes instead.

Spotted Towhee

The Spotted Towhee searches for food on the ground. It hops forward and back, using its feet to rake the leaves away. It finds seeds or insects under the leaves.

Listen for this bird's buzzy, cat-like *mew* call. In the spring, the male flies to the tops of shrubs to sing his song. It sounds a bit like he is singing *drink-your-tea!*

Nests are usually built on the ground or close to it. Chicks leave the nest at about 10 days old, before they can even fly.

Brewer's Blackbird

Brewer's Blackbird is sometimes called the Glossy
Blackbird because of the male's shiny feathers.
The female, though, is a dull gray-brown.

Both males and females puff out their feathers to defend their territory. Often as they do this, they will sing their buzzy song. Males will also puff out their feathers when defending their mate.

In the spring and summer, the Brewer's Blackbird can be found in mountain meadows and around mountain rivers. Nestlings are fed caterpillars and other insects.

Wilson's Warbler

Look for Wilson's Warblers in mountain bushes. They spend most of their time flitting from branch to branch looking for insects.

A group of warblers is called a bouquet of warblers.

This bird's *chip* call sounds a bit like someone blowing a kiss!

Males are bright yellow with a black cap. The female lacks the black cap.

The female builds the nest and incubates the eggs on her own. The male helps with feeding the nestlings.

The Publisher: KidsWorld Books

Library and Archives Canada Cataloguing in Publication

Title: Mountain birds of the West / Genevieve Einstein & Einstein Sisters.

Names: Einstein, Genevieve, 1977– author. | Einstein Sisters, author.

Identifiers: Canadiana (print) 20210097213 | Canadiana (ebook) 20210097329 | ISBN 9781988183305 (softcover) | ISBN 9781988183312 (EPUB)

Subjects: LCSH: Mountain birds—Northwest, Pacific—Identification—Juvenile literature. | LCSH: Mountain birds—Northwest, Pacific—Juvenile literature. | LCGFT: Field guides.

Classification: LCC QL677.79.M68 E46 2021 | DDC j598.175/309795—dc23

Photo credits: Front cover: GettyImages: Harry Collins. Back cover: GettyImages: Paolo-Manzi, DawnKey, RT-Images.

Bird Illustrations: Gary Ross, Ted Nordhagen, Ewa Pluciennik, Horst Krause

Image Credits: From GettyImages: Alberthep, 41; alukich, 40b; Artusius, 34b; BradWolfe, 13a; BrianEKushner, 9b, 26ab; Carlos Aranguiz, 32a; casch, 57b; ChezBriand, 61a; conceptphotos, 46a; creighton359, 44b; Denja1, 22b, 23a; Devonyu, 68a; hannurama, 11ab; Harry Collins, 23b, 42ab,; Ian_Redding, 10a; ian600f, 24; Jeff Huth, 91b; JenDeVos, 71a; Jganz, 36b; kahj19, 13b, 58; Kaphoto, 35b; Karel Bock, 82b; Karine Patry, 81b; Kyle Bedell, 85a; Lynn_Bystrom, 33; Mason Maron, 09, matthewo2000, 22a, MichaelSchmilz, 90, MikeLane45, 8b, mirceax, 35a, 60a, 79a; OldΓulica, 45b; Ondrej Prosicky, 10b; Paolo-Manzi, 28; PaulReevesPhotography, 46b, 72, 88, 89b; photographybyJHWilliams, 8a, 54a; rand22, 83; randimal, 38; RCKeller, 68b; RichardSeeley, 16a; Riverheron, 53a; spates, 65; tami1120, 40a; The_Near_North, 47; through-my-lens, 71b; w-ings, 85b; Wildnerdpix, 52; yhelfman, 87b.Icons: GettyImages: Alexander_Kizilov; ChoochartSansong, rashadashurov, MerggyR, agrino, lioputra, FORGEM, Stevy, Intpro, MaksimYremenko, Oceloti, Thomas Lydell, Sudowoodo. From Flickr: Agust42nto, 75b; Alan Schmierer, 20a, 29b, 56, 64b; Andrey Gulivanov, 29a; Andy Morffew, 36a; Andy Reago & Chrissy McClarren, 48, 62, 67a, 95b; Becky Matsubara, 57a, 64a, 87a, 94; Bettina Arrigoni, 39a; Brette Soucie, USFWS, 19b; Caleb Putnam, 76a; Channel City Camera Club, 18b; Daniel Plumer, 49a; David A Mitchell, 63a; dfaulder, 54b, 80; Don Henise, 67b; Don Owens, 31a; Eric Gropp, 39b; Felix Uribe, 45a; gailhampshire, 12b; Gary Leavens, 76b; Glacier NPS, 73b; Greg Schechter, 34a; Gregory "Slobirdr" Smith, 61b; Howard Cheng, 93a; Jacob W Frank, NPS, 9a, 14a, 43a, 53b, 93b; Jacob W Frank, RMNP, 75a; jeimey31, 20b; Jim Peaco, 59b; Jim Richmond, 32b; John Flannery, 82a; Kaaren Perry, 86; Kate Yates, Bureau of Land Management, 55; Keith Roper, 51; Larry Lamsa, 70; Laura Wolf, 44a; marneejill, 37a; Martyne Reesman, Oregon DFW, 78; Melissa McMasters, 66b; Mike Morel, USFWS, 27; Mike's Birds, 30a, 50b, 59a, 63b; nature80020, 31b; Neal Herbert, NPS, 15; Nick Varvel, 17; Nigel, 79b; Patrick Cashin, Metropolitan Transportation Authority, 43b; Patrick Myers, NPS, 14b; Paul Hurtado, 60a, 84; PEHart, 95a; Peter Plage, USFWS, 12a; pirhan, 79a; Rhona Anderson, 25b; Richard Probst, 30b; Roberto, 49b; Ryan Mandelbaum, 50a; Sandy Brown Jensen, 89a; Sara Giles, USFWS, 37b; seabamirum, 21; Shawn McCready, 92; Shogun X, 60b; Silver Leapers, 18a, 19a, 81a; Steve Colwell, 91a; Tom Koerner, USFWS, 16b; Tony Hisgett, 74; Vic Schendel, USFWS, 25a. From Wikimedia Commons: Jonathon Jongsma, 77.

Icons: GettyImages: Alexander_Kizilov; ChoochartSansong, rashadashurov, MerggyR, agrino, lioputra, FORGEM, Stevy, Intpro, MaksimYremenko, Oceloti, Thomas Lydell, Sudowoodo.

We acknowledge the financial support of the Government of Canada.
Nous reconnaissons l'appui financier du gouvernement du Canada.

Funded by the Government of Canada
Financé par le gouvernement du Canada